Great Works Instructional Guides for Literature

HAMILTON

An American Musical

Music, Lyrics, and Book by Lin-Manuel Miranda
Great Works Authors: Dona Herweck Rice and Emily R. Smith

SHELL EDUCATION

Consultant

Katie Colln, Bellflower Unified School District, California

Contributing Authors

Stephanie Kraus and Kiley E. Smith

Publishing Credits

Corinne Burton, M.A.Ed., *President*; Emily R. Smith, M.A.Ed., *Content Director*; Lee Aucoin, *Senior Graphic Designer*; Stephanie Bernard, *Assistant Editor*; Don Tran, *Graphic Designer*

Image Credits

Getty Images (cover, 1, 25, 37)

Standards

© 2007 Teachers of English to Speakers of Other Languages, Inc. (TESOL)
© 2007 Board of Regents of the University of Wisconsin System. World-Class Instructional Design and Assessment (WIDA)
© Copyright 2010. National Governors Association Center for Best Practices and Council of Chief State School Officers. All rights reserved.

Shell Education

a division of Teacher Created Materials
5301 Oceanus Drive
Huntington Beach, CA 92649-1030
ISBN 978-1-4258-1695-7
https://www.tcmpub.com/shell-education
© 2017 Shell Educational Publishing, Inc.

Table of Contents

How to Use This Literature Guide

Today's standards demand rigor and relevance in the reading of complex texts. The units in this series guide teachers in a rich and deep exploration of worthwhile works of literature for classroom study. The most rigorous instruction can also be interesting and engaging!

Many current strategies for effective literacy instruction have been incorporated into these instructional guides for literature. Throughout the units, text-dependent questions are used to determine comprehension of the text as well as student interpretation of the vocabulary words. The books chosen for the series are complex exemplars of carefully crafted works of literature. Close reading is used throughout the units to guide students toward revisiting the text and using textual evidence to respond to prompts orally and in writing. Students must analyze the story elements in multiple assignments for each section of the book. All these strategies work together to rigorously guide students through their study of literature.

With this particular unit, the study of rigorous text has been taken one step further. Students are asked to analyze, respond to, and interact with content through songs. If possible, students should have the lyrics of the songs in front of them, but all the activities in this guide can be done with only the soundtrack. To further your study of the play, have copies of *Hamilton: The Revolution* by Lin-Manuel Miranda and Jeremy McCarter readily available to students.

The next few pages will make clear how to use this guide for a purposeful and meaningful study of Miranda's astonishing masterpiece. Each section of this guide is set up in the same way to make it easier for you to implement the instruction in your classroom.

Theme Thoughts

The great works of literature and theater used throughout this series have important themes that have been relevant to people for many years. Many of the themes will be discussed during the various sections of this instructional guide. However, it would also benefit students to have independent time to think about the key themes of the play.

Before students begin listening to the songs or reading the lyrics, have them complete *Pre-Reading Theme Thoughts* (page 14). This graphic organizer will allow students to think about the themes outside the context of the story. They'll have the opportunity to evaluate statements based on important themes and defend their opinions. Be sure to have students keep their papers for comparison to the *Post-Reading Theme Thoughts* (page 63). This graphic organizer is similar to the pre-reading activity. However, this time, students will be answering the questions from the point of view of one of the characters in the play. They have to think about how the character would feel about each statement and defend their thoughts. To conclude the activity, have students compare what they thought about the themes before they listened to the songs or read the lyrics to what the characters discovered during the story.

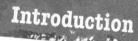

How to Use This Literature Guide (cont.)

Vocabulary

Each teacher overview page has definitions and sentences about how key vocabulary words are used in the section. These words should be introduced and discussed with students. There is also a student vocabulary activity page in each section. Students are asked to define the ten words chosen by the authors of this unit. With the assignment, you may want to have students get into pairs to discuss the meanings of the words. Allow students to use reference guides to define the words. Monitor students to make sure the definitions they have found are accurate and relate to how the words are used in the songs.

On each vocabulary student page, students are asked to answer a text-related question using at least one vocabulary word. The following question stems will help you create your own text-based vocabulary questions if you'd like to extend the discussion:

- How does this word describe _____'s character?
- In what ways does this word relate to the problem in this play?
- How does this word help you understand the setting?
- In what ways is this word related to the solution of the problem in the play?
- Describe how this word supports the play's theme of ....
- What visual images does this word bring to your mind?
- For what reasons might Miranda have chosen to use this particular word?

At times, more work with the words will help students understand their meanings. The following quick vocabulary activities are good ways to further study the words.

- Have students practice their vocabulary and writing skills by creating sentences, paragraphs, or stanzas in which multiple vocabulary words are used correctly and with evidence of understanding.
- Students can play vocabulary concentration. Students make a set of cards with the words and a separate set of cards with the definitions. Then, they lay the cards out on the table and play concentration. The goal of the game is to match vocabulary words with their definitions. Students should add other words from each section to make the game more challenging.
- Students can create word journal entries about the words. Students choose words they think are important and then describe why they think each word is important within the play.
- Have students write couplets or short poems using the words.

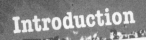

How to Use This Literature Guide (cont.)

Analyzing the Literature

After students have read or listened to the songs in each section, hold small-group or whole-class discussions. Questions are written at two levels of complexity to allow you to decide which questions best meet the needs of your students. The Level 1 questions are typically less abstract than the Level 2 questions. Level 1 is indicated by a square, while Level 2 is indicated by a triangle. These questions focus on the various story elements, such as character, setting, and plot. Student pages are provided if you want to assign these questions for individual student work before your group discussion. Be sure to add further questions as your students discuss what they've heard or read. For each question, a few key points are provided for your reference as you discuss the play with students. (**Note:** For consistency, all answers are provided in the literary present tense based on the play even if the events also really took place in history.)

Reader Response

In today's classrooms, there are often great readers who are below-average writers. Much time and energy is dedicated to reading that little time may be left for writing skills. To help teachers include more writing in their daily literacy instruction, each section of this guide has a literature-based reader response prompt. Each of the three genres of writing is used in the reader responses within this guide: narrative, informative/explanatory, and argument. Students have a choice between two prompts for each reader response. The prompts require students to determine text-to-text connections, to make connections within the text, and/or to focus on historical information shared within the play.

Close Reading the Literature

Within each section, students are asked to closely listen to or reread a specific song. After each close reading (listening), there are text-dependent questions to be answered by students. Encourage students to read each question one at a time and then go back to the song and/or lyrics to discover the answer. Work with students to ensure that they use the lyrics as textual evidence to determine their answers rather than making unsupported inferences. Once students have answered the questions, discuss what they discovered. Suggested answers are provided in the answer key.

How to Use This Literature Guide (cont.)

Close Reading the Literature (cont.)

The generic, open-ended stems below can be used to write your own text-dependent questions if you would like to give students more practice.

- Give evidence from the songs to support ....
- Justify your thinking using textual evidence about ....
- Find evidence to support your conclusions about ....
- What textual evidence helps the reader understand ...?
- Use the lyrics to tell why _____ happens.
- Based on events in the play, ...
- Use textual evidence to describe why ....

Making Connections: Historical, Musical, and Theatrical

The activities on these pages help students make cross-curricular connections to American history, the study of music, and theater. Each of these types of activities requires higher-order thinking skills from students. At times, students will be asked to listen to the songs again, study the lyrics, or conduct further research online. You may consider having students choose from among these three activities in each section. That way, students' personal preferences will be considered.

Creating with the Story Elements

It is important to spend time discussing the common story elements in literature. Understanding the characters, setting, and plot can increase students' comprehension and appreciation of the play. If teachers discuss these elements daily, students will more likely internalize the concepts and look for the elements in their independent reading. Another important reason for focusing on the story elements is that students will be better writers if they think about how the stories they read are constructed.

Students are given four options for working with the story elements. They are asked to create something related to the characters, setting, or plot of the play. For this guide, music has been added as a fourth category. Students are given a choice in this activity so that they can decide to complete the activity that most appeals to them. Different multiple intelligences are used so that the activities are diverse and interesting to all students.

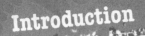

How to Use This Literature Guide (cont.)

Culminating Activity

This open-ended, cross-curricular activity requires higher-order thinking and allows for a creative product. Students will enjoy getting the chance to share what they have discovered through studying the play.

Comprehension Assessment

The questions in this section are modeled after current standardized tests to help students analyze what they've read or listened to and prepare for tests they may see in their classrooms. The questions are dependent on the lyrics and require critical-thinking skills to answer.

Response to Literature

The final post-reading activity is an essay based on the text that also requires further research by students. This is a great way to extend the study of this play into other curricular areas. A suggested rubric is provided for teacher reference.

Correlation to the Standards

Shell Education is committed to producing educational materials that are research and standards based. As part of this effort, we have correlated all of our products to the academic standards of all 50 states, the District of Columbia, the Department of Defense Dependents Schools, and all Canadian provinces.

Purpose and Intent of Standards

The Every Student Succeeds Act (ESSA) mandates that all states adopt challenging academic standards that help students meet the goal of college and career readiness. While many states already adopted academic standards prior to ESSA, the act continues to hold states accountable for detailed and comprehensive standards. Standards are statements that describe the criteria necessary for students to meet specific academic goals. They define the knowledge, skills, and content students should acquire at each level. State standards are used in the development of our products, so educators can be assured they meet state academic requirements.

How to Find Standards Correlations

To print a customized correlation report of this product for your state, visit our website at www.teachercreatedmaterials.com/administrators/correlations/ and follow the online directions. If you require assistance in printing correlation reports, please contact our Customer Service Department at 1-877-777-3450.

Correlation to the Standards (cont.)

Standards Correlation Chart

The lessons in this guide were written to support today's college and career readiness standards. This chart indicates which sections of this guide address which standards.

College and Career Readiness Standards	Section
Read closely to determine what the text says explicitly and to make logical inferences from it; cite specific textual evidence when writing or speaking to support conclusions drawn from the text.	Analyzing the Literature Sections 1–4; Close Reading the Literature Sections 1–4; Creating with the Story Elements Sections 1–4; Post-Reading Response to Literature
Determine central ideas or themes of a text and analyze their development; summarize the key supporting details and ideas.	Analyzing the Literature Sections 1–4; Close Reading the Literature Sections 1–4; Making Historical Connections Sections 1–4; Making Musical Connections Sections 1–4; Making Theatrical Connections Sections 1–4
Analyze how and why individuals, events, or ideas develop and interact over the course of a text.	Analyzing the Literature Sections 1–4; Close Reading the Literature Sections 1–4; Creating with the Story Elements Sections 1–4; Post-Reading Response to Literature
Interpret words and phrases as they are used in a text, including determining technical, connotative, and figurative meanings, and analyze how specific word choices shape meaning or tone.	Understanding Vocabulary Words Sections 1–4; Figurative Language Sections 1, 3; Rhythmic Language Sections 2, 4
Integrate and evaluate content presented in diverse media and formats, including visually and quantitatively, as well as in words.	Making Musical Connections Sections 1–4; Making Theatrical Connections Sections 1–4
Delineate and evaluate the argument and specific claims in a text, including the validity of the reasoning as well as the relevance and sufficiency of the evidence.	Analyzing the Literature Sections 1–4; Close Reading the Literature Sections 1–4
Write arguments to support claims in an analysis of substantive topics or texts using valid reasoning and relevant and sufficient evidence.	Reader Response Sections 1–3
Write informative/explanatory texts to examine and convey complex ideas and information clearly and accurately through the effective selection, organization, and analysis of content.	Reader Response Sections 2, 4
Write narratives to develop real or imagined experiences or events using effective technique, well-chosen details and well-structured event sequences.	Reader Response Sections 1, 3–4

Correlation to the Standards (cont.)

Standards Correlation Chart (cont.)

College and Career Readiness Standards	Section
Produce clear and coherent writing in which the development, organization, and style are appropriate to task, purpose, and audience.	Reader Response Sections 1–4; Post-Reading Response to Literature
Conduct short as well as more sustained research projects based on focused questions, demonstrating understanding of the subject under investigation.	Making Historical Connections Sections 1–4; Post-Reading Response to Literature
Demonstrate command of the conventions of standard English grammar and usage when writing or speaking.	Reader Response Sections 1–4; Post-Reading Response to Literature
Demonstrate command of the conventions of standard English capitalization, punctuation, and spelling when writing.	Reader Response Sections 1–4; Post-Reading Response to Literature
Determine or clarify the meaning of unknown and multiple-meaning words and phrases by using context clues, analyzing meaningful word parts, and consulting general and specialized reference materials, as appropriate.	Understanding Vocabulary Words Sections 1–4; Figurative Language Sections 1, 3; Rhythmic Language Sections 2, 4
Demonstrate understanding of figurative language, word relationships, and nuances in word meanings.	Understanding Vocabulary Words Sections 1–4; Figurative Language Sections 1, 3; Rhythmic Language Sections 2, 4
Acquire and use accurately a range of general academic and domain-specific words and phrases sufficient for reading, writing, speaking, and listening at the college and career readiness level; demonstrate independence in gathering vocabulary knowledge when encountering an unknown term important to comprehension or expression.	Understanding Vocabulary Words Sections 1–4; Figurative Language Sections 1, 3; Rhythmic Language Sections 2, 4

TESOL and WIDA Standards

The lessons in this book promote English language development for English language learners. The following TESOL and WIDA English Language Development Standards are addressed through the activities in this book:

- **Standard 1:** English language learners communicate for social and instructional purposes within the school setting.

- **Standard 2:** English language learners communicate information, ideas and concepts necessary for academic success in the content area of language arts.

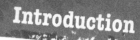

About the Author—Lin-Manuel Miranda

Lin-Manuel Miranda was casually looking around a bookstore one day when he came across *Alexander Hamilton* by Ron Chernow. He bought the bestselling biography and began reading it on vacation in Mexico. After a few chapters, Miranda was hooked. The book describes how Hamilton, an orphan from the Caribbean, wrote his way out of poverty and overcame all odds to shape a new nation. Miranda was inspired. He wanted to bring the Founding Father's journey to life in a new way. He started rewriting the story—this time as a rap and hip-hop musical.

In 2009, just one year after his vacation, the White House held its first ever Evening of Poetry, Music, and the Spoken Word. Miranda was invited to perform, based on his success as a rising star on Broadway. He thought it was the perfect time to try out one of his songs from *The Hamilton Mixtape*, which he would later rename *Hamilton*.

It took Miranda six years to write *Hamilton: An American Musical*. His White House performance helped open some doors to bring it into production for the stage. He asked Thomas Kail to be the director, Alex Lacamoire to be the music director, and Andy Blankenbuehler to be the choreographer. The play opened on Broadway on August 6, 2015.

Hamilton won the Pulitzer Prize for Drama in April 2016. It was the ninth musical to win the prestigious honor since the award began in 1916. Miranda was also nominated for a Pulitzer Prize in 2009 for *In the Heights*, his first musical play.

In 2016, *Hamilton* was nominated for 16 Tony® Awards—Broadway's biggest honor—and won an amazing 11 trophies. The show won the award for Best Musical, and Miranda took home trophies for Best Score and Best Book of a Musical.

Possible Plays/Texts for Text Comparisons

Students would enjoy comparing and contrasting Miranda's play *In the Heights* with *Hamilton: An American Musical*. Both plays are set in New York City, at different times in history. Each tells the story of an immigrant from the Caribbean who is trying to find his way in American culture. Each main character has big dreams and also has to face the realities of everyday life.

Possible Plays for Text Sets

- Aristophanes. 411 BC. *Lysistrata*.
- Edwards, Sherman, and Peter Stone. 1969. *1776*.
- Larson, Jonathan. 1996. *Rent*.
- Lerner, Alan Jay. 1960. *Camelot*.
- Rodgers, Richard, and Oscar Hammerstein. 1949. *South Pacific*.
- Schönberg, Claude-Michel, and Alain Boublil. 1980. *Les Misérables*.
- Shakespeare, William. 1592. *Richard III*.
- Webber, Andrew Lloyd. 1976. *Evita*.

Summary of *Hamilton: An American Musical*

Hamilton: An American Musical, a revolutionary Broadway musical play, opened in the summer of 2015, about 260 years after the real-life Founding Father on whose life it is based was born. The play was an immediate success, breaking theater records and creating a buzz in the theater community and throughout the country unlike anything that had been seen in relationship to a musical. Historical as well as contemporary, the play reveals Alexander Hamilton's life story against the backdrop of the American Revolution and the early evolution of the young nation, all while making the story fully relevant to today's viewing audience.

A Founding Father of enormous significance, the true-life man was all but forgotten by modern audiences. The one factor often remembered was the tragic end of Hamilton's life, in a duel fought with fellow Founding Father, Aaron Burr. Based on the acclaimed *Alexander Hamilton* biography by Ron Chernow, the play tells of Hamilton's life from his difficult youth in the West Indies, through his move to New York City, the years of the Revolution, the early years of the developing country, to Hamilton's untimely death. The story is told in context of other key historical figures, each with relevance to Hamilton's life. Because Hamilton lived the life of a genius whose pen—his skill with words and writing—delivered him from poverty and obscurity to riches and relevance, his story is revealed through modern hip-hop and rhythm and blues music, making a connection to many hip-hop artists whose lives are sometimes seen to follow a similar arc. Essentially, Hamilton is shown as a genius whose drive transforms his life, but whose upbringing and even hubris are fully implicated in his downfall and demise. Burr may shoot him, but Hamilton is his own worst enemy.

Also of significance to Hamilton's story is a group of women in his inner circle, including first his mother, and ultimately branching out to his future wife and champion, Elizabeth Schuyler, and her sister, the brilliant Angelica Schuyler. Because Hamilton's weaknesses are heralded as much as his prowess, a woman deeply involved in Hamilton's eventual disgrace, Maria Reynolds, also plays a key role.

With the exceptions of the actors playing Hamilton, Burr, Eliza and Angelica Schuyler, George Washington, and King George of England, all performers play two roles—one of significance in the revolutionary years and one in the years of the young nation. Perhaps of even more importance, all roles are played without attention to the races or ages of the real-life individuals. In that way, Hamilton's story becomes much more than the story of the man and people who lived so long ago. It is an "American Musical"—at its core, the inclusive story of every American.

Note: There are mature themes and profanity used throughout the songs in this play. Please think about your students before working closely with some of the more mature songs. You should listen to every song and review all activities before completing them with your students.

Cross-Curricular Connection

This play is ideal for making early American history more relevant and meaningful to students. By reading and listening to the songs, students learn fantastic details about many of the country's Founding Fathers.

Summary of *Hamilton: An American Musical* (cont.)

How the Play Is Divided in This Guide

This book is divided into four sections based on the songs in *Hamilton: An American Musical*. This list is provided for easy reference as you prepare your study of the play.

Section 1—Act I, Songs 1–13
- "Alexander Hamilton"
- "Aaron Burr, Sir"
- "My Shot"
- "The Story of Tonight"
- "The Schuyler Sisters"
- "Farmer Refuted"
- "You'll Be Back"
- "Right Hand Man"
- "A Winter's Ball"
- "Helpless"
- "Satisfied"
- "The Story of Tonight" (Reprise)
- "Wait for It"

Section 2—Act I, Songs 14–23
- "Stay Alive"
- "Ten Duel Commandments"
- "Meet Me Inside"
- "That Would Be Enough"
- "Guns and Ships"
- "History Has Its Eyes on You"
- "Yorktown"
- "What Comes Next?"
- "Dear Theodosia"
- "Non-Stop"

Section 3—Act II, Songs 1–9
- "What'd I Miss?"
- "Cabinet Battle #1"
- "Take a Break"
- "Say No To This"
- "The Room Where It Happens"
- "Schuyler Defeated"
- "Cabinet Battle #2"
- "Washington on Your Side"
- "One Last Time"

Section 4—Act II, Songs 10–23
- "I Know Him"
- "The Adams Administration"
- "We Know"
- "Hurricane"
- "The Reynolds Pamphlet"
- "Burn"
- "Blow Us All Away"
- "Stay Alive" (Reprise)
- "It's Quiet Uptown"
- "The Election of 1800"
- "Your Obedient Servant"
- "Best of Wives and Best of Women"
- "The World Was Wide Enough"
- "Who Lives, Who Dies, Who Tells Your Story?"

Name _____

Date _____

Pre-Reading Theme Thoughts

Directions: Read each of the statements in the first column. Decide if you agree or disagree with the statements. Record your opinion by marking an *X* in Agree or Disagree for each statement. Explain your choices in the fourth column. There are no right or wrong answers.

Statement	Agree	Disagree	Explain Your Answer
Everybody has two sides to his or her character: one positive and one negative.			
People should support their families above all else.			
In all situations, you should choose a side and let yourself be heard.			
People should fight for their rights and the rights of others.			

Vocabulary Overview

Ten key words from the songs in this section are provided below with definitions and sentences about how the words are used in the play. Discuss these important vocabulary words with the students. If you think these words or other words in the section warrant more time devoted to them, there are suggestions in the introduction for other vocabulary activities (page 5).

Word	Song	Definition	Sentence about Text
squalor	"Alexander Hamilton"	dirty, bad living conditions	Hamilton grew up in **squalor** and poverty.
bursar	"Aaron Burr, Sir"	the person in charge of money at a school	Hamilton punches the **bursar** at Princeton.
unimpeachable	"My Shot"	trusted, reliable	Hamilton says his "power of speech" is **unimpeachable**!
ascendancy	"My Shot"	a powerful position	Hamilton expects people to see his **ascendancy** in the new government one day.
rabble	"Farmer Refuted"	a group of people who can become violent	Some people think the Patriots are **rabble**.
venerated	"Right Hand Man"	felt a deep respect for someone	The Revolutionary soldiers **venerate** Washington.
scrutiny	"Right Hand Man"	carefully examine something	Washington faces **scrutiny** from a whole country.
askance	"Satisfied"	in a way that shows little trust	Hamilton looks **askance** when Angelica asks about his family.
homilies	"Wait for It"	short talks about religious topics	Burr's grandfather delivered **homilies** in church.
inimitable	"Wait for It"	unable to imitate	Burr calls himself **inimitable** and original.

Name _____

Date _____

Understanding Vocabulary Words

Directions: The following words appear in this section of the play. Use context clues and reference materials to determine an accurate definition for each word. Then, respond to the text-dependent vocabulary question.

Word	Song	Definition
squalor	"Alexander Hamilton"	
bursar	"Aaron Burr, Sir"	
unimpeachable	"My Shot"	
ascendancy	"My Shot"	
rabble	"Farmer Refuted"	
venerated	"Right Hand Man"	
scrutiny	"Right Hand Man"	
askance	"Satisfied"	
homilies	"Wait for It"	
inimitable	"Wait for It"	

1. What qualities of Hamilton make him **inimitable**?

_____

_____

_____

_____

Name _____

Date _____

Figurative Language—Match It!

Directions: Match each figure of speech with the quotation that illustrates it by writing the correct letter on each line. Then, find another figure of speech in the play, and explain how you know it is that type of figurative language.

Part A

Figure of Speech	Example Quotations
_____ hyperbole	A. "I'm a diamond in the rough, a shiny piece of coal." —Hamilton in "My Shot"
_____ idiom	B. "And there's a million things I haven't done." —Hamilton in "Alexander Hamilton"
_____ personification	C. "I'm just like my country" —Hamilton in "My Shot"
_____ simile	D. "Chaos and bloodshed already haunt us" —Hamilton in "Farmer Refuted"

Part B

Example quotation: _____

_____

Figure of speech: _____

_____

How does this quotation illustrate this figure of speech?

_____

_____

_____

Teacher Plans

Analyzing the Literature

Provided below are discussion questions you can use in small groups, with the whole class, or for written assignments. Each question is given at two levels so you can choose the right question for each group of students. Activity sheets with these questions are provided (pages 19–20) if you want students to write their responses. For each question, a few key discussion points are provided for your reference.

Story Element	■ Level 1	▲ Level 2	Key Discussion Points
Character	Describe some of the difficult aspects of Hamilton's early life.	How do Hamilton's difficult beginnings affect his life?	Hamilton is born out of wedlock in poverty. His father leaves when he is 10, and his mother dies when he is 12. He ends up working to save himself. These difficult formative years shape him into a man who does not give up fighting for what he believes. He may be afraid to stop pushing himself because he has seen how hard life can really be.
Setting	How does New York City play an important role in the early scenes of the play?	What role does New York City play in the early part of the American Revolution?	Much of the play takes place in New York City. That bustling city is one of the hubs of the Patriots during the pre-Revolutionary years. Hamilton finds other Patriots to fight alongside. Hamilton fights the British through the city and, in doing so, catches the eye of Washington.
Character	What kind of help does Washington need from Hamilton?	For what reasons does Hamilton not want to work closely with Washington?	Washington needs someone to help strategize and organize. He is "outgunned, outmanned, outnumbered, outplanned." He heard that Hamilton is smart, hardworking, and brave. Hamilton wants to be on the battlefield. He doesn't want to be a secretary concerned with logistics. Hamilton's gift with words is a benefit to Washington.
Plot	How might connecting with the Schuyler family change Hamilton's life?	In what ways is Eliza a perfect spouse for Hamilton?	The Schuyler family is a politically connected family from New York. Mr. Schuyler is a state politician, and his daughters are intelligent Patriots. Hamilton develops a close relationship with both Eliza and Angelica; Angelica challenges him intellectually, while Eliza is a better match for him emotionally. Eliza expects love and respect from him and will support him moving forward.

Name _____

Date _____

■ Analyzing the Literature

Directions: Think about the section you just read. Read each question and state your response with textual evidence.

1. Describe some of the difficult aspects of Hamilton's early life.

   _____
   _____
   _____
   _____
   _____

2. How does New York City play an important role in the early scenes of the play?

   _____
   _____
   _____
   _____
   _____

3. What kind of help does Washington need from Hamilton?

   _____
   _____
   _____
   _____

4. How might connecting with the Schuyler family change Hamilton's life?

   _____
   _____
   _____
   _____
   _____

Name _____

Date _____

▲ Analyzing the Literature

Directions: Think about the section you just read. Read each question and state your response with textual evidence.

1. How do Hamilton's difficult beginnings affect his life?

   _____

   _____

   _____

   _____

2. What role does New York City play in the early part of the American Revolution?

   _____

   _____

   _____

   _____

3. For what reasons does Hamilton not want to work closely with Washington?

   _____

   _____

   _____

   _____

4. In what ways is Eliza a perfect spouse for Hamilton?

   _____

   _____

   _____

   _____

Name _____

Date _____

Reader Response

Directions: Choose one of the following prompts about this section to answer. Be sure to include a topic sentence in your response, use textual evidence to support your opinion, and provide a strong conclusion that summarizes your opinion.

Writing Prompts

Narrative Piece—Research more details about Hamilton's childhood. Then, write a historical fiction piece about a young Hamilton finding his way to New York City.

Argument Piece—In "Aaron Burr, Sir," Hamilton says, "If you stand for nothing, Burr, what'll you fall for?" Using evidence from the first section of the play explain why Hamilton asks this question.

_____

_____

_____

_____

_____

_____

_____

_____

_____

_____

_____

_____

_____

Name _____

Date _____

Close Reading the Literature

Directions: The song "My Shot" took Lin-Manuel Miranda almost a year to write. Closely listen to or reread the song. Read each question and then revisit the song to find evidence that supports your answer.

1. According to the song, what constitutes Hamilton's "shot"?

   _____

   _____

   _____

   _____

   _____

2. In what ways is the United States "young, scrappy, and hungry"?

   _____

   _____

   _____

   _____

   _____

3. Compare and contrast the reasons Lafayette, Mulligan, and Laurens want to take their shots.

   _____

   _____

   _____

   _____

4. Based on the song, why does Hamilton often think about death?

   _____

   _____

   _____

   _____

Name _____

Date _____

Making Historical Connections— King George

Directions: Research the real King George III. Find information about his reaction to the Declaration of Independence. Compare and contrast his real reaction to the reaction shared in "You'll Be Back."

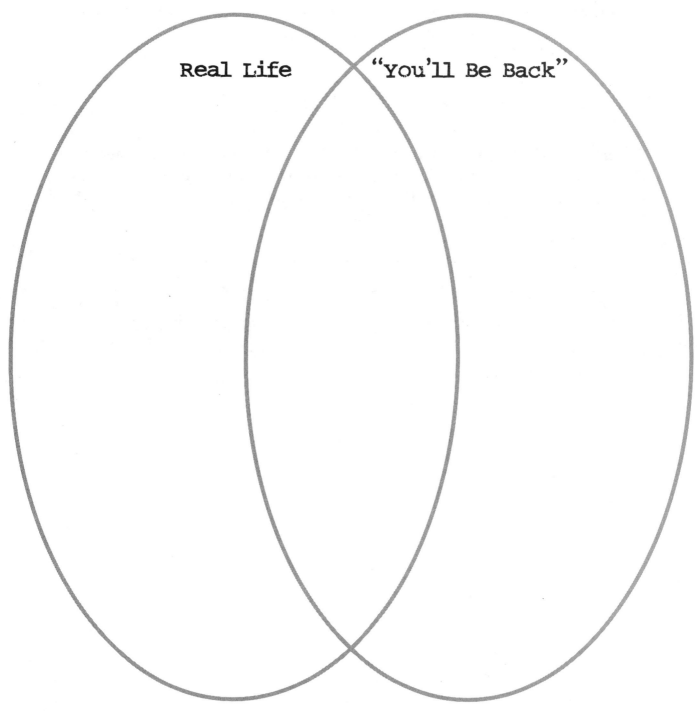

Real Life   "You'll Be Back"

Name _____

Date _____

Making Musical Connections—
"Wait for It"

Listen closely to the song "Wait for It," which Aaron Burr sings in soliloquy. It reveals his inner character and motivation. Pay close attention to the music. Focus on the progression of the song and how the intensity and orchestration build. Thinking about this, what does the music itself "say" about Burr?

Directions: List the lyrics that are emphasized or highlighted in some way through the music. Then, circle three lines that the music "tells" you are essential keys to Burr's character. Finally, sum up Burr in a single word or phrase, based on this song.

_____

_____

_____

_____

_____

_____

_____

_____

_____

_____

_____

_____

_____

_____

Single word or phrase: _____

Name _____

Date _____

Making Theatrical Connections— The Set

Directions: This photograph shows the Hamilton set, which remains mainly the same throughout the show with just a few shifts and changing set pieces. The structure is a skeletal framework used to represent many different things, including a ship's gangplank, a balcony, and a battleground. The floor of the stage includes concentric movable circles, each turning at times in different directions.

1. What is the set meant to convey about the life of Alexander Hamilton?

   _____

   _____

   _____

2. What does it say about the period of history in which he lives?

   _____

   _____

   _____

3. If the set were meant to convey the British perspective, how might it be different?

   _____

   _____

   _____

   _____

Name _____

Date _____

Creating with the Story Elements

Directions: Thinking about the story elements of character, setting, plot, and music in a play is very important to understanding what is happening and why. Complete one of the following activities based on what you've heard or read so far. Be creative and have fun!

Characters

Aaron Burr and Alexander Hamilton have a complicated relationship. Create a graphic flow chart that illustrates the points in this section of the play where they meet. For each meeting, describe where they meet, what happens, and how they feel about each other.

Setting

Pick one song from this section of the play. Draw a picture or a diagram of how you envision the stage design during the song.

Plot

Write a text message conversation between Washington and Hamilton as they discuss whether Hamilton will join Washington's staff. Include strong arguments from Washington to encourage Hamilton to support him.

Music

Describe how two songs from this section are melodically related to one another.

Vocabulary Overview

Ten key words from the songs in this section are provided below with definitions and sentences about how the words are used in the play. Discuss these important vocabulary words with the students. If you think these words or other words in the section warrant more time devoted to them, there are suggestions in the introduction for other vocabulary activities (page 5).

Word	Song	Definition	Sentence about Text
despondent	"Stay Alive"	incredibly sad and without hope	Hamilton says that he has never seen Washington so **despondent** during the war.
camaraderie	"Stay Alive"	a feeling of friendship among a group of people	Laurens and Hamilton show **camaraderie** and bravery together.
contraband	"Stay Alive"	things brought into and out of a country illegally	Hamilton steals **contraband** from behind British lines.
commonplace	"Ten Duel Commandments"	something that happens that is not unique or new	It is **commonplace** to have the "seconds meet face to face" to negotiate during a duel.
battalion	"Meet Me Inside"	a large group of soldiers	Hamilton consistently asks Washington for "command of a **battalion**."
quagmire	"Guns and Ships"	a difficult situation	The Revolutionaries are in a **quagmire** as they fight against Great Britain.
parapet	"Yorktown"	a low wall at the edge of a building or a bridge	The British surrender by raising a flag above a **parapet**.
query	"What Comes Next?"	question	King George has a **query** for the Americans.
mediocrities	"Non-Stop"	things of poor quality	Hamilton wants to expose the **mediocrities** that trouble the new government.
listless	"Non-Stop"	lacking energy	Hamilton gives such a long speech that the other members of the Congress are **listless**.

Name _____

Date _____

Understanding Vocabulary Words

Directions: The following words appear in songs in this section. Use context clues and reference materials to determine an accurate definition for each word. Then, respond to the text-dependent vocabulary question.

Word	Song	Definition
despondent	"Stay Alive"	
camaraderie	"Stay Alive"	
contraband	"Stay Alive"	
commonplace	"Ten Duel Commandments"	
battalion	"Meet Me Inside"	
quagmire	"Guns and Ships"	
parapet	"Yorktown"	
query	"What Comes Next?"	
mediocrities	"Non-Stop"	
listless	"Non-Stop"	

1. How does Washington get the U.S. forces out of the **quagmire** of the war?

_____

_____

_____

_____

Name _____

Date _____

Rhythmic Language Activity

internal rhyme—literary device describing words that rhyme within the same line, words that rhyme from the middles of two lines, or a word at the end of one line that rhymes with the middle of the next line.

Directions: Review the definition and examples of internal rhyme. Then, try your hand at writing your own lines with internal rhyme.

Examples

- "If this is the end of *me*, at least I have a friend with *me*. / Weapon in my <u>hand</u>, a <u>command</u>, and my men with *me*." —Hamilton in "Yorktown"
- "We'll bleed and *fight* for <u>you</u>, we'll make it *right* for <u>you</u>." —Burr in "Dear Theodosia"
- "Why do you *write* like you're running out of <u>time</u>? / Write day and *night* like you're running out of <u>time</u>? / Ev'ry day you *fight*, like you're running out of <u>time</u>." —Burr in "Non-Stop"

Write Your Own!

_____

_____

_____

_____

_____

_____

_____

_____

_____

_____

_____

Teacher Plans

Analyzing the Literature

Provided below are discussion questions you can use in small groups, with the whole class, or for written assignments. Each question is given at two levels so you can choose the right question for each group of students. Activity sheets with these questions are provided (pages 31–32) if you want students to write their responses. For each question, a few key discussion points are provided for your reference.

Story Element	■ Level 1	▲ Level 2	Key Discussion Points
Character	Why does Washington send Hamilton home?	What are the major disagreements between Washington and Hamilton?	Washington and Hamilton disagree about Hamilton's role in the army. Washington needs Hamilton's incredible brain, and Hamilton wants to show his intense bravery. Due to the disagreements on what Hamilton's focus should be, the two men separate during the war. Also, Washington knows that Eliza is pregnant, and he wants to keep Hamilton safe.
Plot	Why does Washington get help from Lafayette and the French during the war?	How do Lafayette and the French help the Americans during the war?	Washington doesn't have the type of financial security required to outfit a strong navy. Lafayette and the French provide the United States with a strong navy to fight against the British during the war. The French provide the naval blockade during the Battle of Yorktown, which leads to the final surrender of the British.
Character	How do Burr and Hamilton feel about becoming fathers, based on "Dear Theodosia"?	Based on "Dear Theodosia," how might being fathers change Hamilton and Burr?	They're both excited to become new fathers and expect great things of their offspring. Both Theodosia and Philip bring about great emotional reactions from their fathers. As both men had absent fathers, they plan to "be around" for their children.
Setting/ Character	How is life in New York City different for Hamilton after the war?	In what ways does Burr and Hamilton's relationship change after the war?	After the war, Hamilton and Burr return to New York and work as lawyers. Hamilton wants to focus on creating a stable fiscal government and getting public support for the Constitution, while Burr wants to focus on moving forward in his life and finding a place for himself in the new government. The relationship between the men is not just about work. The tension comes from their different values and beliefs, too.

■ Analyzing the Literature

Directions: Think about the section you just read. Read each question and state your response with textual evidence.

1. Why does Washington send Hamilton home?

_____

_____

_____

_____

2. Why does Washington get help from Lafayette and the French during the war?

_____

_____

_____

_____

3. How do Burr and Hamilton feel about becoming fathers, based on "Dear Theodosia"?

_____

_____

_____

_____

4. How is life in New York City different for Hamilton after the war?

_____

_____

_____

_____

Name _____

Date _____

▲ Analyzing the Literature

Directions: Think about the section you just read. Read each question and state your response with textual evidence.

1. What are the major disagreements between Washington and Hamilton?

   _____
   _____
   _____
   _____
   _____

2. How do Lafayette and the French help the Americans during the war?

   _____
   _____
   _____
   _____
   _____

3. Based on "Dear Theodosia," how might being fathers change Hamilton and Burr?

   _____
   _____
   _____
   _____
   _____

4. In what ways does Burr and Hamilton's relationship change after the war?

   _____
   _____
   _____
   _____

Name _____

Date _____

Reader Response

Directions: Choose one of the following prompts about this section to answer. Be sure to include a topic sentence in your response, use textual evidence to support your opinion, and provide a strong conclusion that summarizes your opinion.

Writing Prompts

Informative/Explanatory Piece—Research and describe the military strategy Washington, Hamilton, and Lafayette used at the real Battle of Yorktown in 1781.

Argument Piece—Think about the discussion that Burr and Hamilton have about the Constitution toward the beginning of "Non-Stop." Defend either Burr's or Hamilton's opinion on whether to defend the Constitution to the public.

_____

_____

_____

_____

_____

_____

_____

_____

_____

_____

_____

Name _____

Date _____

Close Reading the Literature

Directions: The song "History Has Its Eyes on You" is a moving musical conversation between Washington and Hamilton. Closely listen to the song or reread the lyrics. Read each question and then revisit the song to find evidence that supports your answer.

1. According to the song, what happened the first time Washington was given command during a battle?

   _____

   _____

   _____

   _____

2. What does "history has its eyes on you" mean?

   _____

   _____

   _____

   _____

3. What is the main message that Washington wants Hamilton to remember?

   _____

   _____

   _____

   _____

4. Choose one other line from the song and explain its meaning within the context of the song.

   _____

   _____

   _____

   _____

   _____

Name _____

Date _____

Making Historical Connections— Yorktown

Directions: Conduct further research to discover details about Hamilton's role at the Battle of Yorktown. Then, create a comic that shows six moments from the battle and Hamilton's actions during each one.

Name _____

Date _____

Making Musical Connections— The World Turned Upside Down

Listen closely to "Yorktown (The World Turned Upside Down)." There is a persistent, driving beat throughout most of the song. Where does it escalate? Where does it slow? Where does it stop?

Directions: List four lyrics where a change happens in the left-hand column and the corresponding beat change (escalates, slows, or stops) across from each in the right. Then, star one beat change from the list and write a statement explaining what that change conveys about the character or the situation.

Lyric	Beat change

Statement

_____

_____

_____

Note: This song includes two instances of crude language that may be offensive.

Making Theatrical Connections—
Costumes

Look at these costumes from the original production of the play. On the left is Lin-Manuel Miranda as Alexander Hamilton in traditional dress. On the right is a member of the ensemble who plays many characters with few additions to the costume, including a soldier, an eighteenth century citizen, a guest at Hamilton's wedding, and more. The base costume for the ensemble is a monotone off-white color, and hair is worn in a contemporary style. No member of the cast looks exactly like the real-life person portrayed. Race, age, and gender don't always matter.

Directions: *Hamilton* is subtitled *An American Musical.* How do the ensemble costumes, hair styles, races, ages, and genders support a timeless, inclusive, and particularly American story?

_____

_____

_____

_____

_____

_____

_____

_____

_____

Name _____

Date _____

Creating with the Story Elements

Directions: Thinking about the story elements of character, setting, plot, and music in a play is very important to understanding what is happening and why. Complete one of the following activities based on what you've heard or read so far. Be creative and have fun!

Characters

Think about the meaning of the line "You will come of age with our young nation" in the song, "Dear Theodosia." Create a visual representation that shows the parallels between the growth of a child and the growth of a new nation.

Setting

Create a map of the Battle of Yorktown. Be sure to show the American lines, the British lines, and the French navy.

Plot

Hamilton's internal drive pushes him to "write like he's running out of time." That kind of single-minded focus can be difficult on relationships. Revisit "Stay Alive" and "That Would Be Enough." Then, write a poem from Eliza's point of view describing how she feels as the war ends.

Music

Listen to the beginning of "Yorktown (The World Turned Upside Down)." Pay special attention to Hamilton's internal soliloquy (beginning with "I imagine death…"). Miranda states that this soliloquy "leads [Hamilton] to maturity." Explain how the lyrics and tempo support Miranda's statement.

Vocabulary Overview

Ten key words from the songs in this section are provided below with definitions and sentences about how the words are used in the play. Discuss these important vocabulary words with the students. If you think these words or other words in the section warrant more time devoted to them, there are suggestions in the introduction for other vocabulary activities (page 5).

Word	Song	Definition	Sentence about Text
abyss	"What'd I Miss"	a very deep hole in space	Jefferson thinks that politics are like an **abyss**.
sedative	"Cabinet Battle #1"	something that calms nervousness or excitement	Hamilton's financial plan is the opposite of a **sedative** for the country.
jettison	"Cabinet Battle #1"	voluntarily emptying a ship of its cargo	Hamilton accuses Jefferson of **jettisoning** all his plans.
intransigent	"Cabinet Battle #1"	very stubborn and unwilling to change	Hamilton thinks Jefferson and Madison are being **intransigent**.
polymath	"Take a Break"	someone who knows about many things	Hamilton is a **polymath** through the agility of his amazing brain.
diametrically	"The Room Where It Happens"	holding completely opposite points of view	Madison, Jefferson, and Hamilton are "**diametric'lly** opposed foes."
vacuous	"Washington on Your Side"	showing very little intelligence	Jefferson insults Hamilton by calling him a "**vacuous** mass."
dissidents	"Washington on Your Side"	people who disagree with established systems	People who oppose Washington are called **dissidents**.
zeal	"One Last Time"	a feeling of enthusiasm that makes someone eager	Washington worked for the government with **zeal** for 45 years.
partisan	"One Last Time"	someone who believes very strongly in a cause	The politicians take part in **partisan** fighting.

Name _____

Date _____

Understanding Vocabulary Words

Directions: The following words appear in songs in this section. Use context clues and reference materials to determine an accurate definition for each word. Then, respond to the text-dependent vocabulary question.

Word	Song	Definition
abyss	"What'd I Miss"	
sedative	"Cabinet Battle #1"	
jettison	"Cabinet Battle #1"	
intransigent	"Cabinet Battle #1"	
polymath	"Take a Break"	
diametrically	"The Room Where it Happens"	
vacuous	"Washington on Your Side"	
dissidents	"Washington on Your Side"	
zeal	"One Last Time"	
partisan	"One Last Time"	

1. Name at least two ways that Jefferson and Hamilton are **diametrically** opposed.

   _____

   _____

   _____

Name _____

Date _____

Figurative Language Activity

Directions: Pick one of the following examples of figurative language, and draw a humorous picture of its literal meaning.

- "Madison, you're mad as a hatter." —Hamilton in "Cabinet Battle #1"
- "…sell New York City down the river?" —Burr in "The Room Where It Happens"
- "A game of chess where France is queen and kingless." —Hamilton in "Cabinet Battle #2"
- "He got Washington in his pocket." —Jefferson in "Washington on Your Side"

Analyzing the Literature

Provided below are discussion questions you can use in small groups, with the whole class, or for written assignments. Each question is given at two levels so you can choose the right question for each group of students. Activity sheets with these questions are provided (pages 43–44) if you want students to write their responses. For each question, a few key discussion points are provided for your reference.

Story Element	■ Level 1	▲ Level 2	Key Discussion Points
Character	Where is Jefferson during the American Revolution?	What role does Jefferson play during the American Revolution?	According to "What'd I Miss," Jefferson is in France during the American Revolution. He fights the war with his words rather than with weapons. In reality, he spent much of the war in his home state serving as governor. In both the play and true life, Jefferson serves as U.S. minister to France.
Setting	How does the setting of the play change from Act I to Act II?	For what reasons did Miranda set Act II in New York City?	In Act I, the play is set in New York City and at other locations of the Revolutionary War, including Washington's army camp and Yorktown. All scenes in Act II take place in New York City, which is now the capital of the new country. These scenes take place during Washington's terms as president.
Plot	In what ways does Burr feel left out of George Washington's administration?	How does Burr fit into the political scene surrounding George Washington?	Aaron Burr never receives the respect he thinks he deserves from the other great leaders of his time. He is not part of Washington's Cabinet. He changes political parties and is elected as a senator from New York. The fact that he changes parties to win power surprises and bothers Hamilton, who is so sure of his own beliefs.
Plot	Why does Washington decide not to run for a third term?	How might the new country have been different if Washington had served a third term?	Washington is a visionary who realizes that the country needs change to advance. Unlike Great Britain, America is a democracy. That means that new leaders with new views can work together to move the country forward. Lesser men would not have realized the importance of diverse points of view in a newly forming government.

■ Analyzing the Literature

Directions: Think about the section you just read. Read each question and state your response with textual evidence.

1. Where is Jefferson during the American Revolution?

2. How does the setting of the play change from Act I to Act II?

3. In what ways does Burr feel left out of George Washington's administration?

4. Why does Washington decide not to run for a third term?

Name _____

Date _____

▲ Analyzing the Literature

Directions: Think about the section you just read. Read each question and state your response with textual evidence.

1. What role does Jefferson play during the American Revolution?

   _____
   _____
   _____
   _____

2. For what reasons did Miranda set Act II in New York City?

   _____
   _____
   _____
   _____
   _____

3. How does Burr fit into the political scene surrounding George Washington?

   _____
   _____
   _____
   _____
   _____

4. How might the new country have been different if Washington had served a third term?

   _____
   _____
   _____
   _____

Name _____

Date _____

Reader Response

Directions: Choose one of the following prompts about this section to answer. Be sure you include a topic sentence in your response, use textual evidence to support your opinion, and provide a strong conclusion that summarizes your opinion.

Writing Prompts

Narrative Piece—Write a third-person narrative about the first time Jefferson and Hamilton meet. Describe the setting, what they talk about, and what they think about each other.

Argument Piece—Choose whether you support Hamilton or Jefferson and Madison after rereading or listening to "Cabinet Battle #1." Support your choice with details from the song.

_____

_____

_____

_____

_____

_____

_____

_____

_____

_____

_____

_____

_____

_____

Name _____

Date _____

Close Reading the Literature

Directions: Closely listen to or reread "The Room Where It Happens." Read each question and then revisit the song to find evidence that supports your answer.

1. What compromise is made in "The Room Where It Happens"?

   _____

   _____

   _____

   _____

   _____

2. Based on the song, how does Burr feel about Jefferson and Madison making a deal with Hamilton?

   _____

   _____

   _____

   _____

   _____

3. How does this all-important meeting among the three men get arranged? Use the song to support your answer.

   _____

   _____

   _____

   _____

4. What does Burr mean by saying "I wanna be in the room where it happens"?

   _____

   _____

   _____

   _____

Name _____

Date _____

Making Historical Connections— Cabinet Battle

Directions: Choose a topic that Jefferson and Hamilton disagree on. Research the real historical facts about the topic. Then, write your own rap battle between these two historical figures.

Name _____

Date _____

Making Musical Connections— One Last Time

Listen again to "One Last Time," the song that relates Washington's decision to step down from the presidency. The song begins with a backbeat that goes in and out of syncopation, underscoring the unsettling shift coming to Hamilton's world. When Washington sings, "One last time," a steady rhythm digs in and the melody dominates. It then shifts again to pure melody when Washington sings, "...when I'm gone." Next, there is a marked slowing and shift purely to strings and piano when the actual words of Washington's speech begin. Finally, the drums return and the tempo escalates as Washington sings, "You and I."

Directions: The lyrics marking the four significant musical changes in the song are listed below. Select one lyric and musical shift and explain what they suggest to the listener about Washington, Hamilton, and their relationship to each another.

- "One last time, / Relax, have a drink with me."
- "...when I'm gone. / Like the scripture says..."
- "Though, in reviewing the incidents of my administration..."
- "You and I."

_____

_____

_____

_____

_____

_____

_____

_____

_____

_____

Name _____

Date _____

Making Theatrical Connections— Choreography

Choreography—or orchestrated dance moves—is an essential piece of most musicals. The dance helps to tell the story. Choreographed by Andy Blankenbuehler, *Hamilton* includes a core of hip-hop dance styles with many other techniques. Of his work, Blankenbuehler says, "There's a little bit of everything." For example, in "What Did I Miss?," Jefferson repeats a unique shuffle step that denotes his character's bravado and cockiness. In "The Room Where It Happens," there are classic Broadway dance steps mixed with contemporary hip-hop swagger.

Directions: Look online for clips of the *Hamilton* choreography for inspiration. Then, select about 30 seconds from "What Did I Miss?" or "The Room Where It Happens," and create your own choreography. Illustrate the moves below with stick-figure drawings or perform the moves yourself.

Name _____

Date _____

Creating with the Story Elements

Directions: Thinking about the story elements of character, setting, plot, and music in a play is very important to understanding what is happening and why. Complete one of the following activities based on what you've heard or read so far. Be creative and have fun!

Characters

Create a Venn diagram comparing Jefferson and Hamilton. Think about how to describe their beliefs, political points of view, and personal lives.

Setting

Research Washington's actual cabinet, and draw a diagram showing one of the cabinet meetings. Label all the participants.

Music

Change the tempo in one of the following songs from slow to fast or fast to slow, and describe how it changes the song's meaning: "Take a Break," "The Room Where It Happens," or "Washington by Your Side."

Plot

Read Washington's Farewell Address and summarize it in 10 Tweets or less. Each Tweet must be no more than 140 characters.

Vocabulary Overview

Ten key words from the songs in this section are provided below with definitions and sentences about how the words are used in the play. Discuss these important vocabulary words with the students. If you think these words or other words in the section warrant more time devoted to them, there are suggestions in the introduction for other vocabulary activities (page 5).

Teacher Plans

Word	Song	Definition	Sentence about Text
protean	"The Adams Administration"	able to do many different things	Hamilton is a **protean** leader who has many skills.
ardently	"The Adams Administration"	eagerly support something	People know that Hamilton **ardently** works at his role in the Cabinet.
Creole	"The Adams Administration"	a person of European descent born in the West Indies	Hamilton is called a **Creole** because he was born in the West Indies and had European parents.
speculation	"We Know"	buying and selling something while hoping to make a profit	Jefferson accuses Hamilton of engaging in illegal **speculation**.
embezzling	"We Know"	to steal money when you are trusted with it	Madison, Burr, and Jefferson accuse Hamilton of **embezzling** from the government.
indifference	"Hurricane"	not caring about something	Hamilton believes God answered his prayers with **indifference**.
virtuosity	"Blow Us All Away"	great skill, especially in the performing arts	Philip says he has the same **virtuosity** as his father.
obfuscates	"The Election of 1800"	makes something more difficult to understand	People think Burr ignores questions and **obfuscates**.
equivocate	"Your Obedient Servant"	to deceive someone by being unclear	Hamilton does not **equivocate**; he states his opinions clearly.
methodically	"The World Was Wide Enough"	carefully done	Burr says Hamilton **methodically** fiddles with his weapon at the duel.

Name _____

Date _____

Understanding Vocabulary Words

Directions: The following words appear in songs in this section. Use context clues and reference materials to determine an accurate definition for each word. Then, respond to the text-dependent vocabulary question.

Word	Song	Definition
protean	"The Adams Administration"	
ardently	"The Adams Administration"	
Creole	"The Adams Administration"	
speculation	"We Know"	
embezzling	"We Know"	
indifference	"Hurricane"	
virtuosity	"Blow Us All Away"	
obfuscates	"The Election of 1800"	
equivocate	"Your Obedient Servant"	
methodically	"The World Was Wide Enough"	

1. Why does it bother Jefferson and Hamilton that Burr **obfuscates** his opinions?

_____

_____

_____

_____

Name _____

Date _____

Rhythmic Language Activity

> **slanted rhyme**—literary device in which words have similar but not identical sounds, either through identical consonant matches but differing vowels or differing consonants and identical vowels

Directions: Review the definition and examples of slanted rhyme. Then, write a slanted rhyme for each word below, either in the form of a single word or as a phrase with the same meter (pattern of beats) as the original word.

Examples

- "...in *his taunts.* / Say what? / Hamilton publishes his *response.*" —Burr and Jefferson in "The Adams Administration"
- "An immigrant embezzling our government *funds.* / I can almost see the headline, your career is *done.*" —Burr, Jefferson, and Madison in "We Know"
- "That's when Reynolds *extorted me* / for a *sordid fee.*" —Hamilton in "We Know"

Write Your Own

hurricane _____

_____

revolution _____

_____

Hamilton _____

_____

_____

Jefferson _____

_____

_____

Teacher Plans

Analyzing the Literature

Provided below are discussion questions you can use in small groups, with the whole class, or for written assignments. Each question is given at two levels so you can choose the right question for each group of students. Activity sheets with these questions are provided (pages 55–56) if you want students to write their responses. For each question, a few key discussion points are provided for your reference.

Story Element	■ Level 1	▲ Level 2	Key Discussion Points
Character	According to Hamilton, what is a *legacy*?	How does Hamilton's legacy change shape from "The Adams Administration" to "The World Was Wide Enough"?	A legacy is "planting seeds in a garden you never get to see." In the beginning of this section, Hamilton's legacy is centered on his politics and his writing. By the end of the section, Hamilton realizes he can leave a different kind of legacy by refusing to shoot Burr.
Setting	Why does Philip's duel take place in New Jersey?	What is interesting about the setting of Burr and Hamilton's duel, and how might that affect the parties involved?	Philip says that, "Everything is legal in New Jersey." The setting of a duel should have certain aspects that level the playing field (quiet, flat land, isolated). Further, in Hamilton's case, the setting of his and Burr's duel brings back memories of Philip.
Plot	Why does Congress ask Hamilton to break the tie in the election of 1800?	Do you think Hamilton makes the right choice in supporting Jefferson over Burr? Explain.	Hamilton is a well-respected Federalist who would normally be neutral in choosing a member of the opposite party. Students should support their choices with details from the play or history.
Character	What event encourages Burr to challenge Hamilton to a duel?	How does Burr feel about shooting Hamilton after the duel?	In the election, Hamilton sides with Burr's enemy, Jefferson, which causes Burr to lose the election. After the duel, Burr feels as though he made himself a villain in his blind hatred of Hamilton. He then realizes that he and Hamilton could have shared the spotlight.

Name _____

Date _____

■ Analyzing the Literature

Directions: Think about the section you just read. Read each question and state your response with textual evidence.

1. According to Hamilton, what is a *legacy*?

   _____

   _____

   _____

   _____

2. What event encourages Burr to challenge Hamilton to a duel?

   _____

   _____

   _____

   _____

3. Why does Philip's duel take place in New Jersey?

   _____

   _____

   _____

   _____

4. Why does Congress ask Hamilton to break the tie in the election of 1800?

   _____

   _____

   _____

   _____

Name _____

Date _____

▲ Analyzing the Literature

Directions: Think about the section you just read. Read each question and state your response with textual evidence.

1. How does Hamilton's legacy change shape from "The Adams Administration" to "The World Was Wide Enough"?

   _____

   _____

   _____

   _____

   _____

2. How does Burr feel about shooting Hamilton after the duel?

   _____

   _____

   _____

   _____

   _____

3. How does the setting of a duel affect its outcome?

   _____

   _____

   _____

   _____

4. Do you think Hamilton makes the right choice in supporting Jefferson over Burr? Explain.

   _____

   _____

   _____

   _____

Name _____

Date _____

Reader Response

Directions: Choose one of the following prompts about this section to answer. Be sure to include a topic sentence in your response, use textual evidence to support your opinion, and provide a strong conclusion that summarizes your opinion.

Writing Prompts

Informative/Explanatory Piece—Explain how King George feels about John Adams being elected and how it affects King George's rule.

Narrative Piece—Imagine a conversation you might have with Hamilton after Philip leaves for his duel with George Eacker. What are Hamilton's concerns? What might you say to reassure him?

_____

_____

_____

_____

_____

_____

_____

_____

_____

_____

_____

_____

_____

_____

_____

Name _____

Date _____

Close Reading the Literature

Directions: Closely listen to or reread "Who Lives, Who Dies, Who Tells Your Story?" Read each question and then revisit the song to find evidence that supports your answer.

1. What actions does Eliza take to secure Hamilton's legacy after his death?

   _____

   _____

   _____

   _____

2. After Hamilton's death, what do Jefferson and Madison say about Hamilton's work?

   _____

   _____

   _____

   _____

   _____

3. Eliza asks, "Will they tell my story?" Who is Eliza referring to as *they*?

   _____

   _____

   _____

   _____

4. Which of Eliza's actions separate Eliza's legacy from Hamilton's legacy?

   _____

   _____

   _____

   _____

Making Historical Connections— Comparing Duels

Directions: Research to discover historical details about Philip Hamilton's duel against George Eacker. Then, research Aaron Burr and Alexander Hamilton's duel. Compare and contrast the two duels in this graphic organizer.

Compare & Contrast

Main Topic

Subtopic

Subtopic

Alike

Different

Name _____

Date _____

Making Musical Connections— The Reynolds Pamphlet

The real-life Reynolds Pamphlet is a lengthy document written by Hamilton to clear himself of unjust allegations. But in so doing, he offers full details on a scandal that deeply damages his moral reputation.

The song "The Reynolds Pamphlet" relays the publication of the document and the public's response as well as that of Hamilton's peers. Of note is the fact that most of the song is spoken, while Jefferson repeats two lines of spoken/sung verse, and only Angelica sings fully. Listen to the song closely, noticing what is spoken, nearly spoken, and sung. Consider why each of these is so.

Directions: Analyze one of the following questions:

- Why is this song mainly spoken?
- Why does Jefferson speak-sing a repeated verse?
- Why is Angelica the only one who sings fully?

_____
_____
_____
_____
_____
_____
_____
_____
_____
_____
_____
_____

Making Theatrical Connections—Lighting and Staging

When the first notes of "Burn" are heard, Eliza Schuyler kneels alone in the downstage right corner (the front of the stage to the audience's left). She is cast in a soft spotlight, with just a candlelit lantern by her side. She remains in that spot while, one by one, she burns her letters to her husband.

Theatrical lighting and staging (how actors and set pieces are positioned) are important pieces of how a story is told. They suggest mood and feeling and highlight aspects of the story for the audience to focus on. In "Burn," all eyes are on Eliza, who "burns" emotionally while she literally burns papers on the stage.

Directions: If you were directing a revival of *Hamilton* that must be different from the original. How might you stage and light "Burn"? Illustrate your choices here. Then, briefly explain why you have selected the lighting and staging that you did.

_____

_____

_____

_____

Name _____

Date _____

Creating with the Story Elements

Directions: Thinking about the story elements of character, setting, plot, and music in a play is very important to understanding what is happening and why. Complete one of the following activities based on what you've heard or read so far. Be creative and have fun!

Characters

Draw a three-frame comic strip of King George's role in the play, with each box representing one of his featured songs ("You'll Be Back," "What Comes Next," and "I Know Him").

Setting

Imagine that Hamilton's story takes place in the South rather than New York City. Rewrite a scene from the play in that setting.

Plot

Write a poem that describes the overall history that the play *Hamilton* is telling.

Music

Many styles of music are used in *Hamilton*. If you were to add a song to the play about an event from Hamilton's life that isn't currently covered (for example, when as a teen, he managed a business for which he worked on his own for several months), what event would you choose? What style of music would you use to tell about it?

Name _____

Date _____

Post-Reading Theme Thoughts

Directions: Read each of the statements in the first column. Choose a main character from *Hamilton: An American Musical*. Think about that character's point of view. From that character's perspective, decide if the character would agree or disagree with the statements. Record the character's opinion by marking an X in Agree or Disagree for each statement. Explain your choices in the fourth column using text evidence.

Character I Chose: _____

Statement	Agree	Disagree	Explain Your Answer
Everybody has two sides to his or her character: one positive and one negative.			
People should support their families above all else.			
In all situations, you should choose a side and let yourself be heard.			
People should fight for their rights and the rights of others.			

Name _____

Date _____

Culminating Activity: Who Tells Their Story?

Directions: Think about Lin-Manuel Miranda's perspective on Alexander Hamilton's life. Be inspired by Miranda's musical as you think about other founders' stories.

1. Choose another founding person from early American history.

   _____

2. Research the life and legacy of your chosen person and complete the following details:

   A. Birth and death dates and locations: _____

   _____

   _____

   B. Key peers, friends, enemies, and family members: _____

   _____

   _____

   _____

   C. Four or five major events in his or her life: _____

   _____

   _____

   _____

   _____

   _____

   _____

   D. Major legacies to the United States: _____

   _____

   _____

   _____

   _____

Culminating Activity: Who Tells Their Story? *(cont.)*

Directions: Now it's your turn to become a composer. Pick one of the major events from your chosen person's life. Write a song (or a scene of rhythmic dialogue) that includes details from the event, at least three characters, and is set in the appropriate time period. As an extra challenge, set your words to music and perform them for your class.

_____

_____

_____

_____

_____

_____

_____

_____

_____

_____

_____

_____

_____

_____

_____

_____

_____

_____

_____

_____

Name _____

Date _____

Comprehension Assessment

Directions: Circle the letter for the best response to each question.

1. What are two reasons that Aaron Burr doesn't like Alexander Hamilton?

    A. Hamilton connects with and influences leaders of the time.

    B. Hamilton was born in the West Indies.

    C. Hamilton shows no fear when it comes to choosing sides and sharing his opinion.

    D. Hamilton is an excellent foot soldier.

2. Which of the following is an example of a time when Burr is overlooked directly because of Hamilton?

    E. Angelica: "Burr, you disgust me."

    F. Washington: "Close the door on your way out."

    G. Hamilton: "And I am not throwing away my shot."

    H. Burr: "I'm getting nervous."

3. What does Eliza Schuyler Hamilton want from her husband?

    A. Eliza wants his fame and money.

    B. Eliza wants his time and attention.

    C. Eliza wants his connections to men like Washington and Jefferson.

    D. Eliza wants his plantation.

4. Which song supports your answer to #3?

    E. "That Would Be Enough"

    F. "Meet Me Inside"

    G. "What Comes Next?"

    H. "Right Hand Man"

5. Which of the following lines is evidence that Hamilton is "non-stop"?

    A. Hamilton: "For once in your life, take a stand with pride."

    B. Burr: "How do you write like tomorrow won't arrive?"

    C. Eliza: "The fact that you're alive is a miracle."

    D. Hamilton: "I know I talk too much, I'm abrasive."

Name _____

Date _____

Comprehension Assessment *(cont.)*

6. Explain the significance of the following lyrics.

   Hamilton: "But your man has to answer for his words, Burr.

   Burr: "With his life? We both know that's absurd, sir."

   _____

   _____

   _____

   _____

7. About what two issues do Jefferson and Hamilton disagree?

   A. the new country's debt

   B. supporting Great Britain in a war

   C. Washington's presidency

   D. slavery

8. Which two lines from "Cabinet Battle #1" illustrate one of your answers for #5?

   E. "Welcome to the present. We're running a real nation."

   F. "His plan would have the government assume states' debts."

   G. "These are wise words, enterprising men quote 'em"

   H. "If we assume the debts, the Union gets a new line of credit,"

9. Summarize Hamilton's thoughts as the action freezes while the deadly bullet heads toward him.

   _____

   _____

   _____

   _____

10. Which of the following are true of Hamilton in the moments before being shot? Choose all that apply.

    A. Hamilton thinks about his wife, Eliza.

    B. Hamilton wishes he had been president.

    C. Hamilton worries about his legacy.

    D. Hamilton takes pride in what he's helped create: America.

Name _____

Date _____

Response to Literature: Alexander Hamilton's Legacy

Overview: Alexander Hamilton, the protagonist of the play, spends his life worrying about his legacy. He works "non-stop" to achieve what he thinks is important.

Directions: Think about Hamilton's legacy. Consider these questions:

- Before 2015, how was Hamilton, the real man, remembered in American history?
- Why is Hamilton, the character, a worthy protagonist in a modern musical play?
- Is Hamilton more to be celebrated or pitied? Why?
- Would Hamilton have been as successful as without George Washington? Eliza Schuyler? Aaron Burr?
- Is Hamilton's legacy diminished by his downfalls?

What was Hamilton's legacy and who helped establish it? Write an essay based on the answers to at least three of the preceding questions. Be sure to include evidence from the play or text. Your essay should follow these guidelines:

- State your opinion about Hamilton's legacy.
- Write at least 750 words.
- Include main points, such as those listed in the directions above.
- Draw upon what you learned from reading and/or listening to *Hamilton*.
- Provide a conclusion that summarizes your point of view.

Name _____

Date _____

Response to Literature Rubric

Directions: Use this rubric to evaluate student responses.

	Exceptional Writing	Quality Writing	Developing Writing
Focus and Organization	☐ States a clear opinion and elaborates well. Engages readers from the opening hook through the middle to the conclusion. Demonstrates clear understanding of the intended audience and purpose of the piece.	☐ Provides a clear and consistent opinion. Maintains a clear perspective and supports it through elaborating details. Makes the opinion clear in the opening hook and summarizes well in the conclusion.	☐ Provides an inconsistent point of view. Does not support the topic adequately or misses pertinent information. Lacks clarity in the beginning, middle, and conclusion.
Play and/or Text Evidence	☐ Provides comprehensive and accurate support. Includes relevant and worthwhile text references.	☐ Provides limited support. Provides few supporting text references.	☐ Provides very limited support for the text. Provides no supporting text references.
Written Expression	☐ Uses descriptive and precise language with clarity and intention. Maintains a consistent voice and uses an appropriate tone that supports meaning. Uses multiple sentence types and transitions well between ideas.	☐ Uses a broad vocabulary. Maintains a consistent voice and supports a tone and feelings through language. Varies sentence length and word choices.	☐ Uses a limited and unvaried vocabulary. Provides an inconsistent or weak voice and tone. Provides little to no variation in sentence type and length.
Language Conventions	☐ Capitalizes, punctuates, and spells accurately. Demonstrates complete thoughts within sentences, with accurate subject-verb agreement. Uses paragraphs appropriately and with clear purpose.	☐ Capitalizes, punctuates, and spells accurately. Demonstrates complete thoughts within sentences and appropriate grammar. Paragraphs are properly divided and supported.	☐ Incorrectly capitalizes, punctuates, and spells. Uses fragmented or run-on sentences. Utilizes poor grammar overall. Paragraphs are poorly divided and developed.

The responses provided here are just examples of what the students may answer. Many accurate responses are possible for the questions throughout this unit.

Understanding Vocabulary Words—Section 1: Act I, Songs 1–13 (page 16)

1. Hamilton is **inimitable** because he is ambitious, he writes and reads all that he can, and he is willing to do anything for his legacy.

Figurative Language—Match It!—Section 1: Act I, Songs 1–13 (page 17)

B. hyperbole

A. idiom

D. personification

C. simile

Close Reading the Literature—Section 1: Act I, Songs 1–13 (page 22)

1. Hamilton's shot is the opportunity to join the rebellion and to help fight for the United States' independence. He wants to work and to fight to build a legacy, and he is willing to die if that means freedom for the United States.

2. The United States is "young, scrappy, and hungry" because it is taking its first steps toward becoming its own independent nation. In this way, it is a "young" country. The fact that the people of the United States are joining together for a revolution shows that they are "scrappy and hungry" for change.

3. While all three men are willing to fight in a war and possibly die for their "shots," each of them has different reasons. Lafayette wants to earn freedom for France. Mulligan wants to "socially advance" by joining the rebellion. Laurens wants to use his shot to help end slavery.

4. Hamilton often thinks about death because he comes from a place where people often die young. He does not expect to live long. He feels that life could end at any moment and does not want to waste precious time and opportunity.

Making Historical Connections—King George— Section 1: Act I, Songs 1–13 (page 23)

- **Real Life:** refers to the people of the colonies as his "unhappy people"; uses military might

- **"You'll Be Back":** references Boston Tea Party; says when colonists are gone, he'll "go mad"

- **Similarities:** believes colonies were treated well; "subjects" used to describe the colonists; reminds the people that they had an agreement

Making Theatrical Connections—The Set— Section 1: Act I, Songs 1–13 (page 25)

1. The set conveys that Hamilton is constantly in motion toward his goals. He doesn't stand still but instead moves and takes action.

2. The skeletal framework is a representation of the time in which Hamilton lives because it represents the skeleton of the United States at the time—the frame on which the country is being built.

3. The British perspective might be more elaborate. It might include a parliament building or the inside of King George III's home as some of the main sets.

Understanding Vocabulary Words—Section 2: Act I, Songs 14–23 (page 28)

1. To get the United States out of the **quagmire**, Washington has Hamilton take charge of a battalion. He also has Lafayette and the French help him build a blockade for the battle of Yorktown.

Close Reading the Literature—Section 2: Act I, Songs 14–23 (page 34)

1. Washington led his men "straight into a massacre," and he "witnessed their deaths firsthand." He also made a lot of mistakes and "felt the shame rise in [him]."

2. The phrase "history has its eyes on you" means that what is happening at this time in Hamilton's life will have an important impact on the future of the nation, so it's vital to remember that what happens is written in stone, so to speak. Hamilton will be remembered for what happens, whether it be good or bad.

3. Washington wants Hamilton to know that from that moment on, he will be remembered and possibly judged or criticized for his actions.

4. Example answer: "You have no control: who lives, who dies, who tells your story" means that life and death are unpredictable. People have no control or say in how others will choose to tell the stories of their lives.

Making Theatrical Connections—Costumes—Section 2: Act I, Songs 14–23 (page 37)

The costumes of *Hamilton* support the timeless and particularly American story by having a simple foundation, much like that of the idea of America. The colonists based the idea of a new nation on a simple ideal: freedom. With that as the base, a complex and intricate country and government was built. The mixed-gendered and racially diverse cast is a reflection of what America is today.

Understanding Vocabulary Words—Section 3: Act II, Songs 1–9 (page 40)

1. The two men are **diametrically** opposed on these issues and more: Jefferson is pro-slavery, while Hamilton is against slavery. Jefferson is a Democratic-Republican, while Hamilton is a Federalist. Jefferson is from the South while Hamilton is from the North.

Close Reading the Literature—Section 3: Act II, Songs 1–9 (page 46)

1. The Compromise of 1790, or the Dinner Table Compromise, is made. The decision is made to move the capital to Washington, D.C., and Hamilton gets Jefferson's support for his financial plans.

2. Burr feels as though he is being left out. He is extremely curious to know what went on during the dinner and exactly how the compromise was made.

3. Hamilton approaches Jefferson for help, so Jefferson "arranged the meeting ... the menu, the venue, the seating."

4. Burr means that he simply wants to be present and involved. He does not want to be left out.

Making Musical Connections—One Last Time—Section 3: Act II, Songs 1–9 (page 48)

The lyrics suggest a friendship and ease around one another; Washington's hope for peace and stability for the country (and in his own life) after he steps down; a professional, respectful, but also poignant tone from Hamilton towards Washington; and a sort of celebration on Washington's part as he gets to "go home," but also that he has faith in the country without him.

Understanding Vocabulary Words—Section 4: Act II, Songs 10–23 (page 52)

1. It bothers Jefferson and Hamilton that Burr **obfuscates** his opinions because it makes it seem as though he has no opinion or stance of his own on important matters.

Close Reading the Literature—Section 4: Act II, Songs 10–23 (page 58)

1. She interviews men he fought alongside in the war. She "tries to make sense of [his] thousands of pages of writings."

2. Madison says that Hamilton is not given enough credit for taking the "country from bankruptcy to prosperity." Jefferson says that Hamilton's "financial system is a work of genius."

3. Eliza is referring to people who will survive after her. She might be referring to friends and family, or she might be referring to the future citizens of the United States.

4. The orphanage separates Eliza's legacy from Hamilton's.

Making Historical Connections—Comparing Duels—Section 4: Act II, Songs 10–23 (page 59)

- **Alike:** took place in Weehawken, New Jersey; used the same pistols; both Hamiltons died

- **Different:** In the duel between George Eacker and Phillip Hamilton, the first shot was fired before the count of ten.

- In the duel between Aaron Burr and Alexander Hamilton, the first shot was fired at a count of ten.

Making Musical Connections—The Reynold's Pamphlet—Section 4: Act II, Songs 10–23 (page 60)

It is mostly spoken to suggest and represent the gossip surrounding the publication of the pamphlet. Jefferson speaks in repeated verse to show his joy that Hamilton, whom Jefferson has never been particularly fond of, has ruined any chance of running for the presidency. Angelica is the only one to sing to portray the emotional distress that Hamilton has put on both her and her sister.

Comprehension Assessment (pages 66–67)

1. A. Hamilton connects with and influences leaders of the time; C. Hamilton shows no fear when it comes to choosing sides and sharing his opinion.

2. F. Washington: "Close the door on your way out."

3. B. Eliza wants his time and attention.

4. E. "That Would Be Enough"

5. B. Burr: "How do you write like tomorrow won't arrive?"

6. These lyrics act as a foreshadowing to the duel between Burr and Hamilton. It is ironic that Burr says risking a life in response to ill words is "absurd" because that is the reason for which he later challenges Hamilton to a duel.

7. A. the new country's debt; D. slavery

8. F. "His plan would have the government assume states' debts."; H. "If we assume the debts, the Union gets a new line of credit,"

9. Hamilton thinks about death, his legacy, what he's done for his chosen country, Laurens, his son, Washington, and his wife.

10. A. Hamilton thinks about his wife, Eliza.; C. Hamilton worries about his legacy.; D. Hamilton takes pride in what he's helped create: America.